The Author of My Soul

By Teresa Rollins

TRILOGY

The Author of My Soul

Trilogy Christian Publishers A Wholly Owned Subsidiary of Trinity Broadcasting Network

2442 Michelle Drive Tustin, CA 92780

Rights Department, 2442 Michelle Drive, Tustin, CA 92780.

Trilogy Christian Publishing/TBN and colophon are trademarks of Trinity Broadcasting Network.

For information about special discounts for bulk purchases, please contact Trilogy Christian Publishing.

Trilogy Disclaimer: The views and content expressed in this book are those of the author and may not necessarily reflect the views and doctrine of Trilogy Christian Publishing or the Trinity Broadcasting Network.

Manufactured in the United States of America

10 9 8 7 6 5 4 3 2 1

Library of Congress Cataloging-in-Publication Data is available.

B-ISBN#: 978-1-63769-204-2

E-ISBN#: 978-1-63769-205-9

DEDICATION

To my Jesus, who loved me even when I thought I was unlovable and to the family and friends He has surrounded me with who have done the same.

I love you, and I am forever grateful.

ACKNOWLEDGMENTS

The title of my book has been taken from lyrics to a song that my daughter Ashley wrote as a teenager many years ago. She found solace in singing and writing music and I am so grateful that even in the midst of my messes, she was blessed with a beautiful gift for worship. Words cannot express my gratitude for His ever-present love and care! He really is the author of our souls and He has everything we need to make us whole. The more we know Him, the more we can show Him to others, and He needs to be known. Let us work together to make His love and His message known in the middle of our journeys. He is our beginning and our end, and He should be allowed to be our Lord in the middle.

TABLE OF CONTENTS

PROLOGUE

" 'I tell you, her sins-and they are many-have been forgiven, so she has shown me much love. But a person who is forgiven little shows only little love.' Then Jesus said to the woman, 'Your sins are forgiven.'

The men at the table said among themselves, 'Who is this man, that he goes around forgiving sins?'

And Jesus said to the woman, "Your faith has saved you; go in peace.' "

Luke 7:47-50

True peace. True joy. After these many years, I have learned that peace and joy only come when I let go and let my Jesus have control, and they come through the gratitude that I feel for the things He has done for me. I have been a gossip, a liar, an adulteress, an idolater, and a cheat, and I could go on. But... because of my God's love and the gift of His Son Jesus, I am forgiven, chosen, redeemed, and I am so loved. And so are you, my friend.

My life is a journey, as is yours. We do not determine our beginning path, but as we grow older, we begin to choose which paths we will take and which ones we will avoid. As brothers and sisters in Christ, we are on this journey together, and we are all learning and growing. When I think about the time I have left on this Earth, I want to live. Really live! William Wallace, the famous Scotsman who fought for his country's freedom, has been quoted as saying, "Every man dies, but not every man really lives." How powerful and true! I am fifty-four years old, and I have learned that there is only one way to joyfully live on this journey. It is only by fully trusting in the strength, power, and goodness of my Holy God and my Lord and Savior, Jesus Christ. I have many scars from the earlier years of my journey, and the lessons I learned while sustaining those wounds have only strengthened my resolve to allow my Lord to lead and guide my way during the last years of my life. Since many of my scars are the result of self-inflicted wounds when I deviated from the true path of peace, I want to encourage you my friend, to hold fast to what is lovely, true, and noble. My story is one of love, loss, and redemption, and my heart is filled with gratitude to my Lord and Savior for His forgiveness, His mercy, and His amazing love! May my story inspire you to be fully surrendered to our God, through the beautiful saving grace of our Lord and Savior Jesus Christ. May you look up when you face troubles, and may you truly comprehend and believe how very much you are loved! Let Him be your first love and find peace.

I so wish that I could speak to that young me of long ago. I would have told her that, even in the darkness, there would be beauty, and I would have wrapped my arms around her and told her that there is always hope. Hope in healed hearts, hope in the beauty of future moments, and even the hope of a happy, joy-filled life, but only through the peace and strength of our Lord and Savior, Jesus Christ. I cannot speak to that hurting young woman of long ago, but I can speak to you, and hopefully through my memories and the story of my missteps, you will learn to walk straight and true even in the darkest valleys of your journey. Fear not, my friend. You are not alone. You are never alone.

I would love to be able to share wisdom about how to cope with tremendous loss and the dark veil of grief that accompanies loss (and we will get to that), but this story is not about my wisdom. It is about my foolishness, my selfishness, and sadly, my lack of faith. I would love to share stories of the beauty of my choices during my times of grief, but I have none. My choices were not beautiful. They were sinful and selfish. I not only lost my unborn child and my infant son, but I also lost sight of the One who should have been my first love, and I certainly lost my way. I am hoping that by reading my story, you will truly know in your heart that the only answer is Jesus. He is our comforter, our healer, our peace giver, and our calm anchor in the midst of our storms. I took my eyes off of my Jesus, and herein was my problem.

You see, the problem with many of us, including me, is that we tend to have a difficult time coming to a point in our lives where we truly let go and fully trust in the goodness and sovereignty of our Lord. Especially in the storms when there seems to be no end or resolution in sight. It is so easy to focus on our pain and to forget who is truly in control of every breath we take. I have come to realize the truly amazing peace that comes from being still and resting in God, no matter what is raging around me, and there is great beauty in that rest. I still go to work, spend time with my family, and live my life, but now I am seated and resting in God's goodness and faithfulness. (Thank you Joyce

Meyer for this beautiful revelation!) It has taken me fifty years to learn this truth. I am hoping to help you learn a whole lot sooner and to help you realize just how precious you are to our Savior and how much He wants to help you in your everyday lives and in the horrendous storms that may arise. Psalm 27:1 says, "The Lord is my light and my salvation—so why should I be afraid?" I so wish that I had looked for that light in my dark valley, but I wasn't looking for my Savior. I was looking around. Looking for relief from the pain of grief and rejection, relief from the fear of the future, and the horrible fear of losing my mind in the storm. My prayer for you, as you read my story, is that you will find this rest. This beautiful, peace-filled rest.

You will find many of the Holy Scriptures woven throughout my story, because my words may encourage you, but only the Holy Scriptures have the power to truly change your life. Please allow these scriptures to permeate your heart and fill you with His truth. Then, when darkness arises, you will know to let His Word be your lamp, and His truth will light your way through. With this knowledge, you will be able to confidently rest in the beautiful assurance that you are not alone. He is there, and when you don't have the strength to take one more step, He will carry you. Not around, but through.

> *"The LORD is my light and my salvation—*
> *so why should I be afraid?*
> *The LORD is my fortress, protecting me from danger,*
> *so why should I tremble?*
> *When evil people come to devour me,*
> *when my enemies and foes attack me,*
> *they will stumble and fall.*
> *Though a mighty army surrounds me,*

my heart will not be afraid.
Even if I am attacked,
I will remain confident.

The one thing I ask of the LORD—
the thing I seek most—
is to live in the house of the LORD all the days of my life,
delighting in the LORD'S perfections
and meditating in his Temple.
For he will conceal me there when troubles come;
he will hide me in his sanctuary.
He will place me out of reach on a high rock.
Then I will hold my head high
above my enemies who surround me.
At his sanctuary I will offer sacrifices with shouts of joy,
singing and praising the LORD with music.

Hear me as I pray, O LORD,
Be merciful and answer me!
My heart has heard you say, 'Come and talk with me.'
And my heart responds, 'LORD, I am coming.'
Do not turn your back on me.
Do not reject your servant in anger.
You have always been my helper.
Don't leave me now; don't abandon me,
O God of my salvation!
Even if my mother and father abandon me,
the LORD will hold me close.

Teach me how to live, O LORD.
Lead me along the right path,
for my enemies are waiting for me.

Do not let me fall into their hands.
For they accuse me of things I've never done;
with every breath they threaten me with violence.
Yet I am confident I will see the LORD'S goodness
while I am here in the land of the living.

Wait patiently for the LORD.
Be brave and courageous.
Yes, wait patiently for the LORD."

Psalm 27

As I begin my story, I will preface it by saying that I have made many shameful choices that I used to struggle to hide, but no longer. I am secure in the knowledge that I am a chosen, redeemed, and forgiven child of the Most High King, and I will not cower in shame anymore. And neither should you! Our enemy would like nothing more than to bring up past sins and continually condemn us for our choices. If you have asked our Jesus to come into your life and change your heart and have asked Him to forgive you for your sins, you have been forgiven and He remembers those sins no more. He has separated them from you as far as the east is from the west, and they are gone. Really think about that for a moment. They are gone. Oh, how this makes my heart swell with gratitude!

"And I will forgive their wickedness, and I will never again
remember their sin."

Hebrews 8:12

"The LORD is compassionate and merciful,
slow to get angry and filled with unfailing love.
He will not constantly accuse us,
nor remain angry forever.
He does not punish us for all our sins;
he does not deal harshly with us, as we deserve.
For his unfailing love toward those who fear him
is as great as the height of the heavens above the earth.
He has removed our sins as far from us
as the east is from the west.
The LORD is like a father to his children,
tender and compassionate to those who fear him.
For he knows how weak we are;
he remembers we are only dust.
Our days on earth are like grass;
like wildflowers we bloom and die.
The wind blows, and we are gone—
as though we had never been here.
But the love of the LORD remains forever
with those who fear him.
His salvation extends to the children's children
of those who are faithful to his covenant,
of those who obey his commandments!"

Psalm 103:8-18

Chapter 1

THE BEGINNING

I was raised in a sweet, Spirit-filled church in Tennessee and knew that I loved our Jesus. When I was fourteen, I met a boy at church and fell in love (You may have rolled your eyes right there, but please stay with me). Since he was known to my parents, I was allowed to date, and when I was seventeen, we married. He had joined the military by this time, and we moved away to Maryland and began our married life. I missed my parents, but everything was new and exciting, and I remember being happy and content. A few months after we were married, he received orders to serve a tour of duty overseas. Our time in Maryland flew by, and he left to serve in South Korea in 1985. The first few weeks were very difficult, but we then discovered that I could go overseas as well if we could find housing off of the military post, so I joined him in August of that year. I enjoyed the time there and found it to be truly eye opening to live with the people and cultural norms of another country. I felt that our marriage was strong, and my memories from this period are good.

When his time overseas was over, we returned to another base in Maryland and enjoyed being young, naïve, and married. When his time in the military was over, we moved to south Georgia to live with my mother-in-law, who was one of the godliest and kindest women I have ever had the privilege of knowing. We stayed there for a summer, and then my husband got a job as a police officer in south Florida. We made the move and the huge transition to a new state and community. I became pregnant within a month of our move, and after much illness and even hospitalization for morning, afternoon, and night sickness, we were blessed with a beautiful baby girl. She continually brings joy to my world, and I am so grateful for her! Her name is Ashley Renee, and her very presence makes my heart smile.

I loved being a mom, and I was so happy with our little family. I became pregnant again when Ashley was around twenty-two months old, and we were so excited to welcome a new baby. However, I was extremely ill again with this pregnancy, and I had started to have horrible dreams. When we went in for a regular four-month checkup and ultrasound, our world turned upside down. The technician was talking and laughing with us and then became very quiet. She excused herself and told us that the doctor would like to speak to us in his office. My doctor informed us that our baby had died and that I would have to have a surgical procedure to remove the baby. I started to weep in his office, and I don't remember his words, but I do remember his kindness. I found out on a Friday, but the surgery was not scheduled until the following Wednesday. We went home in a fog and a large sense of shock.

My husband was stoic, but kind. He had been extremely loving and helpful during the first pregnancy with Ashley, but I had been so ill with this second pregnancy that it had weighed on our relationship. I went to church the Sunday after I found out about the baby, and I remember, while standing in the balcony, the congregation started singing, "Because He Lives, I Can Face Tomorrow," and I started to weep. I wish that I had known the power in those precious words at that time. I now know that we can truly face each tomorrow, simply because He does live, and He loves us with an everlasting love. If I had been more mature in my faith, I would have realized that those words could have given me strength, but my focus was not on Him. It was on my pain, and unfortunately, this became a pattern for me on my journey. Selfishly trying to alleviate my pain without the peace and guidance of the Holy Spirit. I was so foolish! If we are going to be salt and light to this world, we must steadfastly hold to the truths in the Bible and live them out in the good times and the bad. I have failed at this so many times on my journey, but my Jesus has been so faithful, even though I have not.

You see, during those early years of our marriage, we had gone to church sporadically and tried to be faithful. However, I viewed our heavenly Father through the eyes of religion, and I felt as if His love was based on my behavior. Somehow, while growing up, I had internalized that His love for me depended on my choices, and if I remained a good girl, I was in good standing with Him. I became a good little rule keeper and strived not to lose the approval of my Savior. My Jesus was my Savior, but I had not allowed Him to be Lord. I was still sitting on the throne of my heart because I didn't view Him with a grateful heart but with fear and trepidation. My fear of Him was not based on reverence but more on my fear of failing and losing His love. What a horrible way to live! We must be careful of the religious rules we place on ourselves, because we can become good little Pharisees if we are not on guard. We can develop a haughty and judgmental attitude if we are not careful as well. I can remember many times during the early part of my journey thinking, "I would never do that!", and then later finding out that was a lie. I ended up doing the very same thing that I had judged someone else for. No one is without sin, and we cannot navigate this walk on our own. True holiness comes from the gratitude we feel for our God's saving grace and forgiveness through His Son Jesus, and this in turn makes us want to please Him and honor Him. Holiness has nothing to do with our good deeds or strength. It is totally depending on our Holy God to work through us with His divine Holy Spirit and asking Him to lead, guide, and direct. He is the one who is holy.

"Pride leads to disgrace, but with humility comes wisdom."
Proverbs 11:2

I had the surgery to remove my baby and went home to heal. I was distraught with grief, and I was floundering. My husband was wonderful and tried to help, but we did not know how to stop the hurt. I had wanted to move back to Tennessee for a while because I had missed my family, and, during this time, my husband told me to get him applications for the police departments in my home state so he could apply. I jumped at the opportunity and did so. The horrible problem with this was that my husband absolutely loved his job in Florida and did not want to move to Tennessee. He was only showing love to me. I was so lost in my grief that I became self-centered and selfish in trying to make the pain stop, and I didn't process his pain or his true feelings about these choices. I believe this was the beginning of a seed of resentment and bitterness in our marriage. You see, during this time in my journey, I relied on my feelings to help me make my choices. I did not know the importance of asking our God for wisdom and discernment, and I would pay a price for my ignorance. God gives us biblical truths and parameters to help us to stay safe and at peace. They are lovingly given, but many times ignored. Please earnestly pray about every choice you make, especially the ones that can be life changing. Ask for wisdom and discernment, and He will freely give; please do not make pivotal choices when you are hurting.

"So be careful how you live. Don't live like fools, but like those who are wise. Make the most of every opportunity in these evil days. Don't act thoughtlessly, but understand what the Lord wants you to do."

Ephesians 5:15-17

"If you need wisdom, ask our generous God, and he will give it to you. He will not rebuke you for asking."

James 1:5

We moved to Tennessee, and I was thrilled to be back in my hometown and near my parents. My husband started at the new police department and hated it. It was a much smaller town than he was used to, and he was bored and used to joke that his arm got tired of waving. He worked third shift, and he became miserable in his job. In my happiness at being back home, I took his feelings for granted and started to heal from the grief. I became pregnant again, and this made things much better for him because we found out that we were having a boy, and he was so excited about having a son. I was very ill again and struggled the first few months, so my doctor prescribed a medication to help with the nausea and sickness. We went to the regular checkups, and everything seemed to be normal with the pregnancy. During this time, my husband was even hired at a larger police department and seemed much happier, so life was good! Or was it?

What really makes life good? In my immaturity, I believed my happiness was based on my circumstances and the people around me. Through many years of learning, I have come to realize a good life is based on truly putting God first in each of our choices and trusting in His love and care in everyday life and in the storms. Our joy comes from the peace we find in Him. Precious friend, if you are seeking peace, He is your answer. He is your only answer.

I started to notice a difference in my husband's attitude after he began his new job. He seemed more hardened and less empathetic. Part of this may have been the resentment that was brewing, but I also knew that his job as a police officer was extremely difficult. Having the very people that you are trying to protect curse you, fight with you, and continually be on the defensive with you is draining and can lead to a callous attitude if a police officer is not on guard. Law enforcement is a noble and honorable career, but the pay is low, the criticism is high, and the temptations are numerous. The men and women who protect us need our constant prayers. May our God bless them and keep them. They are His servants, and He has given them a career based on honor and service. (I realize that some of you may currently have a different view of these servants, but I humbly ask that you sadly recognize that in every profession there are individuals who harbor ill will in their hearts and do evil in the sight of God and man. This is wrong and should not be tolerated, but we as believers should not judge an entire profession of dedicated men and women based on the evil actions of a few. The honorable ones who serve in law enforcement stand in the gap for us each day. They put themselves in the line of danger so that we and our families can be safe, and I personally feel tremendous gratitude for that service.)

"Everyone must submit to governing authorities. For all authority comes from God, and those in positions of authority have been placed there by God. So, anyone who rebels against authority is rebelling against what God has instituted, and they will be punished. For the authorities do not strike fear in people who are doing right, but in those who are doing wrong. Would you like to live without fear of the authorities? Do what is right, and they will honor you. The authorities are God's servants, sent for your good. But if you are doing wrong, of course you should be afraid, for they have the power to punish you. They are God's servants, sent for the very purpose of punishing those who do what is wrong. So, you must submit to them, not only to avoid punishment, but also to keep a clear conscience."

Romans 13:1-5

My pregnancy progressed, and on Monday, December 2nd, 1991, our son Wesley Alan was born by cesarean section. He weighed eight pounds and fifteen ounces, and he was beautiful! Within minutes of his birth, however, we knew something was terribly wrong. They had lowered him down beside my head so that I could see him and then immediately began to work on him because he was bluish in color. They took him away and reassured us that they would take care of him. Time passed and my husband went to check on him and then came back and told me that there were several people working on him.

They took me to a room, and after waiting for two hours, they came to tell us that our baby son had been born with only half of his heart. The left two chambers were missing. The name of the condition was Hypoplastic Left Heart Syndrome, and our little boy could not live with only half of his heart. The leading pediatric cardiologist informed us that our baby was going to die. He was too weak to wait for a transplant, and he was not a candidate for a second option of multiple surgical repairs. He didn't have enough heart tissue. Our joy turned to mourning, and a nightmare began.

Chapter 2

THE DARKNESS

The next morning, they brought my son to me, and they let me hold him for the first time. I remember saying, "He is so real." I believe this was said because the previous twenty-four hours had seemed surreal, and I had hoped they had been a bad dream. When I held him and touched him, I felt the full force of knowing he was going to die. My heart broke, and I started to feel helpless. I don't remember praying or asking God for healing. I simply remember loving my baby so much and wanting him to live. He had an IV in his head and another in his hand, and he was beautiful. My sweet baby. He was born on Monday, and we spent the week with him, holding him and loving him. We were due to take him home on Friday to let him die peacefully at home, but on Friday morning, his nurse came in very early and told us that he would not make it through the day. We held him, and I sang to him about how Jesus loved him and how Jesus loves the little children. Our little boy died Friday afternoon, and we held his silent, still little body for the last time. I wanted to scream and yell, but only silent tears fell as we handed him over to the nurse to be prepared for burial.

Our pastor had never conducted a child's funeral and suggested a quick graveside service. In hindsight, this was not a wise choice for us, but our pastor was a wonderful man who only had the best intentions. You see, we needed to have a time to mourn with family and friends, but this did not happen. We simply met at the cemetery the next day and said our goodbyes.

My father was a police officer in our small town, and some of his friends escorted Wesley's hearse in their patrol cars as it made its way from the funeral home to the cemetery. I still remember that act of kindness, because I felt like those kind men were honoring our son, showing love and support for us and our baby.

I have seen video clips of people grieving in other countries. Of wailing and raw grief. I felt like screaming and grabbing hold of that small white casket, but I did not. I simply stood in a haze of grief and wept. For some reason, outward expressions of grief seem to be the norm for others, but not in our country. I find this sad, and I truly believe that our norm can actually be harmful in some cases to those who are grieving. We need to remember that we will all grieve differently and that it is important that each one of us feels the freedom to do so. We are simply to love and support one another, not to judge.

Our pastor said some kind words over Wesley's small white casket, and we sang "Jesus Loves the Little Children." Our closest family and friends had joined us, and afterward, we hugged and cried, and I remember feeling their love and kindness.

One of my aunts had kept Ashley for me during the graveside service, and after the service concluded, we thought it might be best to remove all remembrances of Wesley. (I know

now how foolish this was, but we had no idea what was best at the time.) You see, we had put Wesley's crib and baby items in Ashley's room and had built her up as being the big sister. During his time in the hospital, she hadn't understood the sadness and had started to become withdrawn in her sadness. I was so consumed; I didn't realize what pain my little girl was feeling. That afternoon after the service, my husband and my uncle started to take down the crib, and Ashley started to wail and cry and ran into the bathroom and actually cowered under the bathroom sink. She had never acted like that before, and we simply did not understand how to help her or even begin to process all the emotions that came with grief. Her daddy coaxed her out and held her as she cried. I cannot put into words the feelings of helplessness at that time. My baby had died, and I didn't know how to help my other baby to deal with this storm.

That first night was probably one of the most difficult because it tore us up to think of our little baby being in the cold, hard ground. We buried him on December 7th, and it was extremely cold. All I could think of was my baby being in his small, white casket alone.

One of the few beautiful moments during this time came on the Monday morning after we buried Wesley. A very kind, older man came to our home early that morning and brought us cinnamon rolls in a pan. He worked at the funeral home that had taken care of Wesley and had made an effort to bring us breakfast. The beauty was not in the cinnamon rolls, but in his love. His simple act of kindness touched our hearts, and we started to realize how our God works through the hearts and hands of His people to bless others when hearts are hurting.

My husband and I saw beauty through the love and support of our church, our close family, and our friends. We spoke about Wesley at first, but as days turned into weeks, we spoke about him less and less. We could simply look at each other and feel the pain. At first, we visited the cemetery every day, but time went by and the visits became less frequent. I started to feel like I was shattered inside and wanted to wail and scream but felt like this was unacceptable, so I would beat my fists on the wall in the shower so no one would know that I didn't have it all together. For some reason, I felt like I needed to smile and be normal in public, so other people would not feel uncomfortable with my grief. I realized that in their kindness, they didn't know what to say, and it would become awkward; so I just pretended that I was great, and life was good. I buried my grief and tried to stay busy to forget. I had started taking classes again at the local college within weeks of Wesley's death and had tried to revive some normalcy. I would see acquaintances that I had been in class with the previous semester who knew about Wesley's death and I would just smile and pretend that all was well in my world, but it wasn't.

"Laughter can conceal a heavy heart, but when the laughter ends, the grief remains."

Proverbs 14:13

A few weeks into the semester, I was sitting in a Geology class, and the professor was lecturing when I started to cry. I couldn't stop, and I had to get up and leave the class. I truly felt like I was losing my mind. I consulted the doctor who had delivered Wesley, and she prescribed an anti-depressant for me. I started on the medication, and it did help me to get the crying under control. However, I did not like the way I felt while taking it, so I only took it for a few weeks.

I learned that there is no forgetting the pain in your time of grief. I now know that we need to feel it, acknowledge it, and ask our sweet Lord to help us to feel His peace in the midst of it. If you are reading this and you are currently in the midst of grieving, I can promise that you will begin to find your way without your loved one, but your love and longing for them will remain in your heart forever. Our precious Lord will help you to find your joy once again even as you begin the rest of your earthly journey without them, but you need to ask Him for help and strength. He is your way to peace. He is our only way to peace. Alcohol, drugs, promiscuity, excessive shopping, etc. may all temporarily mask the pain, but in the end, they will only multiply it and make things much worse. Jesus is your healer and restorer. Let Him heal you by drawing near to Him.

"He heals the brokenhearted and bandages their wounds."

Psalm 147:3

My husband tried to be kind and supportive, but he was struggling too. We began to speak about having another baby, but we knew that was not to be. Due to the extreme morning sickness with each of my pregnancies, we had agreed for me to have a tubal ligation during the cesarean that was performed for Wesley's birth. We both knew there would be no more babies for us. We were caught in a tangle of grief, and I was losing hope. My husband was too, but I was too selfish to realize the extent of his pain. One of the sad facts about grief in our society is that we women get most of the comfort from others, and our men are taught to be stoic and strong. How wrong this is! Our men hurt too, and they should be allowed to show it. Due to our norms, I believe a lot of men cover their hurts with anger, and this can become a problem for them and for those they love.

He had gone back to work at the police department soon after Wesley died, and our lives went on. If we had been communicating during this time, things might have been different, but our mutual grief kept us apart, and due to our following choices, we would be pulled further apart and eventually torn asunder.

Around June, I noticed he was more withdrawn and seemed less tender with me. I used to tease him that I was going to check his collar for lipstick or smell his uniform for perfume. I think I knew subconsciously that something was wrong, but my trust was complete, and I never doubted his faithfulness. However, in late July, things got worse, and I knew something was wrong. He told me in early August that he was in trouble and needed to leave for a few days. I didn't understand, but I was worried about him; so I agreed, and he left. We spoke by phone for a couple of days and then I told him that he needed to come home, and he agreed to come and talk. Looking back, I believe that I knew the truth, but my heart couldn't bear that truth.

When I got home that day, he was in our den. He was subdued and quiet. I simply asked him if there was someone else, and he put his head in his hands and shook his head yes. I cannot describe to you the feelings that rushed through me at that time, but I would not wish them on anyone. Sadly, many of you reading this know exactly how I felt. You would think that I would have told him immediately to leave, but I loved him, and I wanted him to stay, so I told him so. I told him that we could work through it, but he told me there was more. We were upstairs in the bedroom by this time, and he was packing his clothes. I thought, *More, how could there be more?* Then I realized, and I asked if she was pregnant. He simply shook his head yes, and my world shifted. Our baby had died eight months prior, and now he was leaving me to have a baby with another woman. Something broke in me at that moment, and I am sad to say that, due to my following choices, I was broken for a very long time.

Chapter 3
THE RUNNING

I found out that he had met his new love at work. She had been a waitress in a restaurant he had visited while on duty. Coincidentally, the very same surgeon who had informed us that our baby could not live with half of his heart had performed a life-saving surgery on this woman. (How cunning our enemy can be... Conversations started... Intimacies shared... Affairs begun.) She was ten years younger than me, and she was beautiful. Because he had left me to be with her, I felt ugly, rejected, and so alone. My trust was broken, and sadly, my moral compass broke as well. All I could think of was making the pain go away because it seemed unbearable. I truly think my mind shut out every inch of logical thinking, and I was fully focused on the feelings of rejection and loss. I lost hope, and I lost my way.

Edgar Allan Poe is quoted as saying, "I was never really insane except upon occasion when my heart was touched." My heart had been touched and torn, and I let that pain rule my thoughts as well, and I foolishly relied on myself to mend the damage. This, my friend, is not the way God intended for us to walk through our trials.

I so wish that I had looked to my Jesus for help and comfort and not to the sinful ways of this world. I should have sought

God's wisdom, but I only sought relief from the nightmare. Please note that seeking worldly ways to relieve our pain or escape from our problems only compounds our situations and can lead to our ultimate lowest points and sometimes even our destruction. Our enemy knows this, too, and we should always be on guard. Especially in our darkest moments.

I would like for you to pause for just a moment and think about the exchange that I just revealed between Ashley's father and myself when he told me about the affair. Let's view it through spiritual eyes. Our Holy God watching these revelations and their consequences with eyes filled with compassion and love for His beloved children because He loves us so much, and the evil one watching as well with glee and triumph in his eyes because of the hatred he feels for us. Isn't it time to stop letting our mutual enemy triumph in our earthly battles? We are at war, my friend, and we have the victor on our side. It is time to start acting like victors! It is time to stand.

"Be on guard. Stand firm in the faith. Be courageous. Be strong.
And do everything with love."
1 Corinthians 16:14

I wasn't on guard, and I wasn't standing firm in the faith. I was lying prostrate on the floor in a fleshly mess of grief. I certainly wasn't courageous or strong, and I let fear take over and this made me weak. Take up your shield of faith, my friend, and fight with God's help. You were not meant to fight alone. You have a helper who is waiting for your call!

"A final word: Be strong in the Lord and in his mighty power.
Put on all of God's armor so that you will be able to stand firm
against all strategies of the devil. For we are not fighting against
flesh-and-blood enemies, but against evil rulers and authorities of

the unseen world, against mighty powers in this dark world, and against evil spirits in the heavenly places.

Therefore, put on every piece of God's armor so you will be able to resist the enemy in the time of evil. Then after the battle you will be standing firm. Stand your ground, putting on the belt of truth and the body armor of God's righteousness. For shoes, put on the peace that comes from the Good News so that you will be fully prepared. In addition to all of these, hold up the shield of faith to stop the fiery arrows of the devil. Put on salvation as your helmet, and take the sword of the Spirit, which is the word of God.

Pray in the Spirit at all times and on every occasion. Stay alert and be persistent in your prayers for all believers everywhere."

Ephesians 6:10-18

Again, I had no idea how to handle this life event with Ashley. When her dad first left, I told her that he had gone on vacation to explain his absence. (Trust me, I know you are saying, "Really?", and I agree. I was lost!) When his absence progressed and he didn't come home, she began to cry for him, especially at night. I used to kneel beside her bed as she cried out loud, "Daddy, daddy." I would cry silently as she called out for him. I hated the feelings of helplessness and hopelessness that I felt, and I started to feel hatred for my rival as well. I could not change things for my little girl, and since I could not take away her pain, I started to assign blame. Frankly, I was losing it, and my sweet girl was in the middle of a horrible grown-up mess.

One afternoon during this time, my doorbell rang, and it was a couple from church. They told me that they had bought some groceries for us and asked if I would accept them. They brought in bag after bag of food for Ashley and me. I was deeply touched by their kindness, and to this day, I am grateful. I only wish that I had realized they were showing my Jesus' love for me by being His hands and feet. He was showing His ever-present love and care through their act of kindness, but it was not enough for me to fully trust Him. He was constant, but I was moving away. My eyes were on myself and my circumstances, and I just wanted the pain to stop.

A family member's friend asked me out, and I started to date another man. Obviously, I was not standing firm in faith or kneeling in prayer. My sole focus was on me and not on my helper. I knew it was wrong, but the sting of rejection was raw, and the attention was flattering, and I walked into a pit. I was still married and still in love with my husband, but I made a choice based on selfishness and fear, and I stepped into a mess of sin. Again, please do not make pivotal choices when you are hurting. Our enemy will send temptations when we are the most vulnerable, and his aim is to steal, kill, and destroy. Do not let him! He almost succeeded with me. I let him steal my joy, kill my dreams, and destroy my witness for a very large part of my journey.

Looking back at this next part of my story, I wonder who I even was, but I will tell this part with the perfect peace that I am forgiven, and no stones will be thrown. I was drowning in pain, fear of the future, and a horrible view of myself as rejected and unwanted. You see, I didn't understand the all-encompassing love of our Father and that He is our comfort, our provider, and our beauty. I so wish that I had! Looking back, my wish for simple relief from the darkness of pain led me into further darkness, and my sinful choices began to plant the roots of despair.

"Those who are dominated by the sinful nature think about sinful things, but those who are controlled by the Holy Spirit think about things that are pleasing to the Spirit. So letting your sinful nature control your mind leads to death. But letting the Spirit control your mind leads to life and peace."

Romans 8:5-6

I was trying to numb the gnawing pain even if only for a short time, but because of my choices, I became adrift in guilt and shame and self-condemnation as well. I started to despise myself, and I felt dirty and unworthy. I didn't feel like a "good girl" anymore, and I learned through this mess that, when we start to feel guilt, shame, and condemnation, we sometimes let go of our truth and sink deeper into sin. I now know that I was never "good." The Bible says that my righteous acts are as filthy rags to our God. The only good in any of us is the precious Holy Spirit of God living and breathing and shining on others through our witness. However, in my belief system at that time, I thought that I had to be good to be loved by my Jesus. I now know that is a lie from the pit. His love for us is not based on our choices. He loved me even when I thought all was lost, and He loved me even in the midst of my mess.

"If a man has a hundred sheep and one of them wanders away, what will he do? Won't he leave the ninety-nine others on the hills and go out to search for the one who is lost? And if he finds it, I tell you the truth, he will rejoice over it more than over the ninety-nine that didn't wander away! In the same way, it is not my heavenly Father's will that even one of these little ones should perish."

Matthew 18:12-14

I did not call out to my redeemer, my rescuer, the only One who could help, and my sins swept me away. Are you drowning right now? Are you lost? Call out! Cry out, sweet beloved of God. He is waiting with open arms, and He loves you so much!

I had lost hope, and I was truly in despair. I could not see the light, and I became selfish and self-centered again as I lost sight of my Jesus and my privilege of being a mother to my precious girl. Our enemy loves to tell us that, once we have trashed our lives, there is no hope, but he is a liar! I did not understand God's enormous love for me during this time, but now that I do, I realize that even in my darkest moments of shame, my Heavenly Father was waiting for me, the prodigal. He was waiting with His arms open wide and His grace in abundance. He loves you, too, my friend, and His arms are open for you as well.

Beautiful Words from our Jesus

"In the same way, there is joy in the presence of God's angels when even one sinner repents." To illustrate the point further, Jesus told them this story: "A man had two sons. The younger son told his father, "I want my share of your estate now before you die." So his father agreed to divide his wealth between his sons. "A few days later this younger son packed all his belongings and moved to a distant land, and there he wasted all his money in wild living. About the time his money ran out, a great famine swept over the land, and he began to starve. He persuaded a local farmer to hire him, and the man sent him into his fields to feed the pigs. The young man became so hungry that even the pods he was feeding the pigs looked good to him. But no one gave him anything.

"When he finally came to his senses, he said to himself, "At home even the hired servants have food enough to spare, and here I am dying of hunger! I will go home to my father and say, "Father, I have sinned against heaven and you, and I am no longer worthy of being called your son. Please take me on as a hired servant."

"So he returned home to his father. And while he was still a long way off, his father saw him coming. Filled with love and compassion, he ran to his son, embraced him, and kissed him."

Luke 15:10-20

There is more to this story that you can read, but I want to draw your attention to the father's response to his son's homecoming. The father didn't wait for his son to reach him. He actually ran to meet him because he was so happy to see him. The father's heart was filled with love and compassion for his wayward son. Our Heavenly Father feels the same way about us. His arms are open, His eyes full of compassion, and His mercy and grace are boundless! If you are reading this and you are adrift in guilt and shame, it is time to accept your Heavenly Father's love and head home! His arms are open for you, and He is waiting.

Chapter 4

THE REMNANTS

Within days of my divorce being final, my husband married the woman that he had left me for, and very soon after that, I married the man I was seeing. I knew it shouldn't be, but I seemed powerless to stop it. (Please note that I felt powerless, but I was not. I could have asked our Holy God for help and guidance, but I did not trust Him enough, so I made extremely foolish choices.) I was afraid, and I had lost hope and this man offered me kindness and financial security. It was a pivotal choice in my life, and I have deep regrets, but he was good to my daughter and for that I will always be grateful.

We started to have problems immediately due to my insecurities and my feelings of having made a huge mistake. My heart had not healed from my brokenness and I had married out of a deep sense of shame and an overwhelming fear of the future. I felt worthless, and I made sinful choices that reflected it. How foolish! (When we truly know who we are in Christ, we can stand tall and strong with His help through any battle that is waged. Stand strong in Him sweet friend!) Instead of looking to my Savior for help, I looked around at the world, and I sank deeper into self-loathing. The extreme insecurity that I felt was new to me, and I didn't realize it at the time, but it became forefront in my thoughts because I was so afraid of feeling rejected again. Foolishly, I thought my worth and value were tied to the love and approval of a man. He was an extrovert and wanted to socialize and hug everyone, and having just come from my experience, it was a nightmare. I would become hurt and angry, then we would argue, and I would end up hating the insecurity that I felt. The strife was continual, and I was drowning. Again, I should have looked to my Jesus.

I finally went to see a lovely Christian counselor for help, and she read Psalm 51 with me. It speaks of David's horrible pain and regret over his choices of adultery with Bathsheba and murder of Uriah, and it resonated in my soul. She asked if I truly believed that my Jesus had forgiven me for my sins, and I answered yes. She then asked if I had forgiven myself, and I quickly answered no. I started to weep with the true realization of how I felt about myself. She told me that I wanted everyone to like me, because I was so afraid that, if they saw the real me, they would recoil in horror. I realized that I loathed myself due to my recent life choices, and the guilt, shame, and regret were eating at my soul. Very lovingly, she explained that my beautiful Jesus is sovereign and not me. His forgiveness trumps everything, even my foolish and selfish feelings. He loves me even when I feel unlovable. And He loves you the same.

"Have mercy on me, O God,
because of your unfailing love.
Because of your great compassion,
blot out the stain of my sins.
Wash me clean from my guilt.
Purify me from my sin.
For I recognize my rebellion;

it haunts me day and night.
Against you, and you alone, have I sinned;
I have done what is evil in your sight.
You will be proved right in what you say,
and your judgement against me is just.
For I was born a sinner—
yes, from the moment my mother conceived me.
But you desire honesty from the womb,
teaching me wisdom even there.

Purify me from my sins, and I will be clean;
wash me, and I will be whiter than snow.
Oh, give me back my joy again;
you have broken me—
now let me rejoice.
Don't keep looking at my sins.
Remove the stain of my guilt.
Create in me a clean heart, O God.
Renew a loyal spirit within me.
Do not banish me from your presence,
and don't take your Holy Spirit from me.
Restore to me the joy of your salvation,
and make me willing to obey you.
Then I will teach your ways to rebels,
and they will return to you.
Forgive me for shedding blood, O God who saves;
then I will joyfully sing of your forgiveness.
Unseal my lips, O Lord,
that my mouth may praise you.

You do not desire a sacrifice, or I would offer one.
You do not want a burnt offering.

The sacrifice you desire is a broken spirit.
You will not reject a broken and repentant heart, O God."

Psalm 51:1-17

And the beautiful peace that will come once we release our life to Christ can be summed up in these verses:

"Dear children, let's not merely say that we love each other; let us show the truth by our actions. Our actions will show that we belong to the truth, so we will be confident when we stand before God. Even if we feel guilty, God is greater than our feelings, and he knows everything.

Dear friends, if we don't feel guilty, we can come to God with bold confidence. And we will receive from him whatever we ask because we obey him and do the things that please him.

And this is his commandment: We must believe in the name of his Son, Jesus Christ, and love one another, just as he commanded us. Those who obey God's commandments remain in fellowship with him, and he with them. And we know he lives in us because the Spirit he gave us lives in us."

1 John 3:18-24

Her wise counsel helped me temporarily, but I still did not rest in Him. I did not have total belief and trust in His love, goodness, and sovereignty. I continued to try to heal myself and tried to make my marriage work, but the constant strife weighed on my soul. To everyone on the outside, we probably seemed like a happy couple because he didn't dwell on the conflicts, and I would just smile and pretend that everything was right in the world when it wasn't. I left our marriage in 2004, and we divorced in 2006. I cried the day it was final because I felt like such a failure. I had felt like a failure for a very long time.

Please notice that there were eight I's in that one paragraph. If we continually rely on ourselves and try to live this life on our own, we will not live in victory and joy. The Holy Spirit is our helper, and we need to stop pushing Him to the back of the boat. He needs to be allowed to lead and be the one in control of the steering and guiding the course for our lives.

Ashley and I moved into an apartment and started our new normal. Again, I had created hardship for my daughter. I know that she has loved me through each moment of her life, but respect is earned, and I cannot blame her for that struggle. I think she perceived me as weak in many ways, and I believe she was right. If I had allowed God to be the real source of my strength throughout my journey, her life might have been vastly different. I think one of the main reasons that forgiving myself had been so difficult was because, once I started to emerge from the veil of grief, I realized how much my selfish choices had impacted my precious daughter. Our enemy loves to bring up our "if only" thoughts, and sometimes they can be a torture. Let them go, sweet friend. Our God loves you and wants you to live in victory and joy, and this can only be done by daily relying on Him and trusting in His mercy, His forgiveness, and His goodness. We serve a good God!

My girlfriends were so exceedingly kind to me during all this mess, and I will always love them for it. We started to attend Bible studies together, and they were always kind and encouraging. They loved me as our Jesus does, with hearts of compassion and kindness. I felt His love through them. Through those studies and the gentle prodding of the Holy Spirit, I started to truly heal and realized that I was not just a shame filled, rejected sinner with no hope. I came to understand that, even though I didn't have the princess story that many of us dream of, I had my story, and with my Jesus' help, I could live in that story and still find joy in Him. I could be His daughter. The King of king's daughter. I started to honestly believe that I am a daughter of the Most High, and my name is written in the precious Lamb's Book of Life. My name. Not my choices.

"And I will be your Father, and you will be my sons and daughters, says the LORD Almighty."

2 Corinthians 6:18

The years passed, and I continued to grow in the beautiful knowledge of God's love and presence. These were some of the happiest for Ashley and me. She was a teenager, and we did have some of those mother/daughter moments, but we were both growing and maturing. She into a confident young woman, and me in my faith. I began to truly heal and realized that I needed to forgive others in order to be free from the past. There had been many moments in the previous years when I had thought that I had already let this go, but there were many instances in Ashley's life when there were struggles, causing me to go back and feel angry about the choices that had been made by those who were charged with nurturing and protecting her, including me. Joyce Meyer says that wisdom is making choices today that you will be happy with tomorrow. Please remember that your children will also live with the choices you make today in their tomorrows as well. Make your choices based on the truth in God's Word. I made some pivotal life choices out of selfishness, fear, and pain, and they caused extreme hurt for my daughter. Please don't do the same.

Chapter 5
THE FREEDOM OF FORGIVENESS

It was not difficult for me to forgive Ashley's father because I knew that many of his hurtful choices had been made during a season of grief. I also knew that he was sorry about the wounds that he had caused because he had apologized years earlier during one of our rare conversations. I harbored no ill will toward him. He will always have a special place in my heart because he is the father of my children, and I will always be grateful for the time that we shared. I truly wish beauty for him.

The next part was harder. Forgiving the woman whom I had blamed for so much hurt. The other woman. This was a struggle, but this is where I needed to learn about perfect love and put it into practice. I had to use empathy and think about what my choices might have been in similar circumstances if I had experienced her upbringing and had a similar life story. This was not to justify her choices, but to help me to see her through the eyes of my Jesus. To see her as a young woman seeking love and value in this sometimes cruel and darkened world. It is not my place to judge. I am to forgive those who trespass against me. The small hurts and the large.

Now, I admit this was not easy. She had called me years earlier and apologized. I had told her in that moment that I forgave her, but in hindsight that was a lie. My heart was not forgiving at that time. I spoke the words, but my heart was still filled with bitterness and resentment. Oh, my friend, those feelings will eat us up and can lead to a very hard heart if we are not careful. A hardened heart can lead us to make very hurtful and even harmful choices to those we target and even those we love. Please do not let the enemy triumph! A hardened heart is sinful, ugly, and destructive. You may be thinking that I have no idea what someone has done to you or to someone you love dearly and that is true, but… It is time to let go, and with His help, this can be done. Let it go and be released from your anger, your bitterness, your hatred. Be free. Our precious Jesus died for that freedom, and it is a free gift from Him to you and to your children and, yes, even to your enemies. I know that our God has forgiven me, and I need to do the same for others. I know that there is no peace for us when we harbor anger, resentment, or unforgiveness in our hearts. I refuse to be held captive by these peace stealers anymore. I want to honor our God and forgive, and so should you, my friend. Forgive. Free yourself and live in peace.

> "Since God chose you to be the holy people he loves, you must clothe yourselves with tenderhearted mercy, kindness, humility, gentleness, and patience. Make allowance for each other's faults, and forgive anyone who offends you. Remember, the Lord forgave you, so you must forgive others. Above all, clothe yourselves with love, which binds us all together in perfect harmony. And let the peace that comes from Christ rule in your hearts. For as members of one body you are called to live in peace. And always be thankful.
>
> Let the message about Christ, in all its richness, fill your lives. Teach and counsel each other with all the wisdom he gives. Sing

psalms and hymns and spiritual songs to God with thankful hearts. And whatever you do or say, do it as a representative of the Lord Jesus, giving thanks through him to God the Father."

Colossians 3:12-17

You may be curious about Ashley's father and his wife today, and I am truly happy to say that they are still together and have several beautiful children. Ashley adores her siblings, and this makes my heart happy. There were challenges for her during her younger years in dealing with divorce and blended families, but our God is faithful, and today she has a beautiful relationship with her father, her stepmother, and her precious siblings. There is peace. Beautiful peace.

Once I truly forgave those who had hurt me on my journey and made a conscious effort to let go of the past and the "if only" regrets, something began to change in me. The more I read about God's love and His beautiful forgiveness and mercy, I began the process of forgiving myself, and I began to like who I was in Him. This was transforming and I actually began to like who I was when I viewed myself though the lens of my Jesus' eyes. I learned through this part of my journey that we cannot truly love others as we should until we love ourselves. Not in a vain, selfish, worldly way, but in knowing our worth and value in Jesus Christ. Oh, the freedom that this knowledge brings!

I read the story of the adulteress woman, and I started to realize just how very much I am loved even when I fail. My beautiful God is love. He loves me even when my choices are not so loveable because He loves me as His child, and I know the power and depth of parental love. There is not a choice that my daughter could make that would take away my love for her. Nothing. Period. And that is how we are loved sweet friend! When our Holy God looks at us, He does not see the ugliness of our sins. He sees the merciful and glorious robe of righteousness that covers us because of our relationship with His Son Jesus. Our precious Lord Jesus. He was wounded so that we could be healed and crucified so that we may have life. There is no love greater than this! Confess your sins and let them go. Let them go! There is now no more condemnation to those who love Christ Jesus.

"Jesus returned to the Mount of Olives, but early the next morning he was back at the Temple. A crowd soon gathered, and he sat down and taught them. As he was speaking, the teachers of religious law and the Pharisees brought a woman who had been caught in the act of adultery. They put her in front of the crowd.

'Teacher,' they said to Jesus, 'this woman was caught in the act of adultery. The law of Moses says to stone her. What do you say?'

They were trying to trap him into saying something they could use against him, but Jesus stooped down and wrote in the dust with his finger. They kept demanding an answer, so he stood up again and said, 'All right, but let the one who has never sinned throw the first stone!' Then he stooped down again and wrote in the dust.

When the accusers heard this, they slipped away one by one, beginning with the oldest, until only Jesus was left in the middle of the crowd with the woman. Then Jesus stood up again and said to the woman, 'Where are your accusers? Didn't even one of them condemn you?'

'No, Lord,' she said.

And Jesus said, 'Neither do I. Go and sin no more.'"

John 8:1-11

Did you notice that at the end of this story, the only two left from the large crowd were the woman and Jesus? He is all that matters, my friend. The haters walked away, and the crowd faded away. It's all about Jesus and the beautiful sacrifice that He made for you and for me. It is time to stop throwing stones. It is time for us to embrace our God-given commission to tell others about our Jesus and to do it in love.

Oh, how I wish I had understood the depth of this love years ago when I was in the dark valley. How I wish that I had leaned on my Savior for direction and had allowed Him to truly be the Lord of my life instead of a passenger as I chose the direction for the relief of my pain. We don't have to smile and pretend that everything is okay when it isn't. We have our Lord's permission to be real, to feel pain, to acknowledge our hurts, our failures, and our deepest, darkest fears. He is our Risen King, and He is also our friend. This life is not about religion. It is about our relationship with our Holy God through His precious Son, Jesus Christ. Either we truly trust and rest in Him, or we keep holding tightly to the reins of our life and we keep trying to steer the course. His course is the only one that is right, wise, and true. There will be painful times, but you will not be alone. He will uphold you with His righteous right hand, and He will under-gird you with strength for your journey and indescribable peace in the midst of your storms. The loss of a loved one, the loss of your good health, the loss of a job, the leaving of a prodigal, the rejection of a spouse. He is the calm in your storm. Please do not start to look around as I did. Look up, my sweet friend. Your help is waiting for you to call. He is waiting with mercy and grace and unfathomable love!

"I will praise the LORD at all times.
I will constantly speak of his praises.
I will boast only in the LORD;
let all who are helpless take heart.
Come, let us tell of the LORD'S greatness;
let us exalt his name together.

I prayed to the LORD, and he answered me.
He freed me from all my fears.
Those who look to him for help will be radiant with joy;
no shadow will darken their faces;
In my desperation I prayed, and the LORD listened;
he saved me from all my troubles.
For the angel of the LORD is a guard;
he surrounds and defends all who fear him.

Taste and see that the LORD is good.
Oh, the joys of those who take refuge in him!
Fear the LORD, you his godly people,
for those who fear him will have all they need.
Even strong young lions sometimes go hungry,
but those who trust in the LORD will lack no good thing.

Come, my children, and listen to me,
and I will teach you to fear the LORD.
Does anyone want to live a life
that is long and prosperous?
Then keep your tongue from speaking evil
and your lips from telling lies!
Turn away from evil and do good.
Search for peace, and work to maintain it.

The eyes of the LORD watch over those who do right;
his ears are open to their cries for help.
But the LORD turns his face against those who do evil;
he will erase their memory from the earth.
The LORD hears his people when they call for help.
He rescues them from all their troubles.
The LORD is close to the brokenhearted;
he rescues those whose spirits are crushed.

The righteous person faces many troubles,
but the LORD comes to the rescue each time.
For the LORD protects the bones of the righteous;
not one of them is broken!

Calamity will surely overtake the wicked,
and those who hate the righteous will be punished.
But the LORD will redeem those who serve him.
No one who takes refuge in him will be condemned."

Psalm 34

I have heard many people say that sometimes our spiritual journey will bring us full circle in order to teach us a lesson that we are having trouble learning or to bring new blessings to light. I was about to learn my most important lesson on my journey about perfect love and trust. I was in my forties and experiencing true joy and peace in my walk with our Lord. I loved being a mom to Ashley, and I felt fulfilled and grateful for my career helping children. Plus, I was so very grateful for my loving family and friends. I felt like our Lord had planted a seed years earlier to help others when I had visited the lovely counselor who had imparted such love and wisdom to me. I had become an elementary school counselor, and my sole desire was to be a help to those little ones in my care. To help each one to feel loved and special and to teach about kindness and integrity and true courage. You may be thinking, "You? With your past?", and I would say, "Yes." Our God does not use perfect people for His mission. There simply aren't any. He uses those of us who know Him and love Him, and many of us have a past that we are not proud of. But our God is a God of forgiveness and mercy and unfathomable love! Oh, how I love Him! Sometimes, those of us who have messed up the most truly grasp the deep importance of the lessons. Through our Lord's redemption, some of our deepest wounds will lead to true wisdom.

What an honor to be entrusted with the task of helping little ones who are so precious to our Holy Creator! What is your task my friend? Are you grateful? Do you truly understand that He will strategically place you in situations, in careers, where you can be a light to draw others to Him? I have heard it said that no hurt is ever wasted, and I believe it. The Bible tells us that all things work for the good of those who love our Lord, and I can now stand on that promise.

> *"And we know that God causes everything to work together for the good of those who love God and are called according to his purpose for them."*
>
> Romans 8:28

> *"For we are God's masterpiece. He has created us anew in Christ Jesus, so we can do the good things he planned for us long ago."*
>
> Ephesians 2:10

Our good works do not save us, but they can help to save others. Our service, our good works, should flow from a grateful heart and a desire to honor our Heavenly Father. His perfect love should be allowed to shine through us in order to draw others to Him. Show His love, sweet friend. Shine His light. Wherever He has placed you, be a light and draw others from their darkness. Let them know through your witness that there is hope, and that peace is within their reach if they will just call out to our Jesus. So many in our world are seeking peace, but they are lost and cannot find their way. Be the salt that makes them thirsty, and then let His love and His light working through you lead them home.

Chapter 6

THE LIGHT

One weekend when Ashley was home from college, I received a voicemail message from a friend who had gone through a divorce the previous year. He was in a rough place and asked if I would take a walk with him. I immediately put up a guard and told Ashley that I could not do that. I had not dated in years and had no plans to do so. Ashley encouraged me to go and told me that he may need to talk. That his request was for a walk, not a date. She understood that sometimes men have a difficult time expressing their feelings to others, and she thought that he may need to talk to someone who had shared similar experiences.

I ended up going on a walk with him, and during that walk, we spoke about the pain of divorce. I encouraged him to let his heart heal before he dated anyone. I shared some of my huge missteps and told him that he needed time to heal. I spoke to him about asking God for wisdom and strength, and I encouraged him to totally rely on Him for his peace and direction. We spoke of his eleven-year-old son and how he was handling everything, and we also spoke about the infant daughter that he had lost years earlier to the same heart condition as my son. My friend's name was Glenn.

Glenn and I continued to meet for walks with each other and with other friends. He worked in law enforcement which brought back many memories from the past, and I spoke to him about the temptations he may face and how he was vulnerable while healing. We were already friends, but as time passed, I started to admire his sense of honor and his deep committed love for his son. My feelings started to change, and I realized that I was falling in love. This was confusing and very surprising, especially when I learned that he felt the same. When we spoke about our reality, we were both concerned about what had come to fruition. What would our children think, and what would the future hold? My thoughts also tended to bring concern about what others would think. (Some of you reading this part may be feeling a little judgmental yourself, but I lovingly ask that you stay with me.)

We began to go on dates, and the more time I spent with him, the more peace I felt. I truly felt like his love was a blessing from God and a comfort to my heart. We married in 2011 in a simple ceremony with only our children and family in attendance. We settled into family life, and we were happy. His son would come and live with us every other week, and we learned a new normal. I had found it ironic and a little disconcerting that he worked in law enforcement and in my naïveté, I didn't realize that our God was about to teach me one of the most important lessons we can learn as Christians. Commandment number one. True trust. Holy trust. Glenn was so attentive and generous with his compliments and appreciation when we started dating and during the first few months of marriage, but as in most marriages, this wanes a little as time goes on. (You sweet ladies know what I mean.) Well, I didn't realize that I still had insecurities from past hurts, and they reared their ugly head quickly. I knew how some women could be flirty with an attractive man in uniform, and when I witnessed it with Glenn, fear rose within me and I became ugly in my actions. I felt like I could not bear the pain of rejection again, and the enemy had a heyday with my thoughts. "What if you are not enough again? What if he meets someone younger? Someone beautiful?" I began to question his actions and his motives. I let my fears start to make me a mess again, and I started making our marriage messy as well. With my fears in the forefront of my thoughts, there was no peace for me or Glenn. Poor Glenn. He was not used to dealing with insecurity and wasn't quite sure how to handle it or me. At first, he was sweet and reassuring, but after a while, he became angry and defensive. Who could blame him? An insecure woman can be ugly and nagging and, boy, was I was ugly! (And maybe a little nagging... He would probably say I did a lot of nagging, but let's continue.)

My daily thoughts would tend to be something like, "What if...? I wouldn't be able to bear that! What can I do to stop it?" These thoughts were consuming. Notice the I's had started again. I was so afraid of feeling the familiar pain of rejection that I became selfish and self-centered again. (Please notice that my pattern of sinful choices was based on my fears because my focus was on them and not on the only One who could ease them.) I wanted to control everything, but I had no control, and I knew it. The tensions continued to grow, and I let fear reign supreme.

After months of strife, I finally realized it, and I realized that I was pushing Glenn away with my worries. If we are not careful with our choices, sweet friend, we can create the very thing that we fear, and our enemy can just sit back and smile in victory.

I knew the problem was inside of me and I knew that it was fear, but the more I tried to reason it away, the bigger it became. I truly didn't think that I could handle the pain that I had felt years earlier again, but through the grace of God, I also knew that Glenn was faithful to me and genuinely loved me. I finally stopped steering the boat and asked for help.

I took my eyes off of myself and the fears, and I focused them on Jesus. I began to read my Bible more and prayed for peace and wisdom, and one day, one sweet day, I realized what I was missing. What I had been missing my entire spiritual walk. I had placed Glenn as my first love. Above all else. Even above God. This is the very same thing I had done in my first marriage. When Ashley's father left, I had felt like my world had ended and I couldn't go on. I had felt like my total identity was tied to our relationship and not to the Holy One who had gifted me with that relationship. God showed me that in order for me to have true peace, He would have to have first place in my heart. Above all else. Our God is love and so very loving and forgiving, but the Bible tells us that He is also a jealous God and seeks our whole heart. As a matter of fact, the first two commandments in the Old Testament lay the foundation for us.

"I am the LORD your God, who rescued you from the land of Egypt, the place of your slavery.

You must not have any other god but me.

You must not make for yourself an idol of any kind or an image of anything in the heavens or on the earth or in the sea. You must not bow down to them or worship them, for I, the LORD your God, am a jealous God who will not tolerate your affection for other gods. I lay the sins of the parents upon their children; the entire family is affected—even children in the third and fourth generations of those

who reject me. But I lavish unfailing love for a thousand generations
on those who love me and obey my commands."

Exodus 20:2-6

And in the New Testament…

"Seek the Kingdom of God above all else, and live righteously,
and he will give you everything you need."

Matthew 6:33

We can see that this is so true! If we are placing ourselves
and our fickle feelings first in our choices, then strife will reign
supreme. Furthermore, if our spouse, our children, our money,
our careers, our entertainment (and I could go on), come before
our God, then there will be constant turmoil and no underlying
peace. He must have first place in our hearts, in our minds, and
in our souls. It is true that all these beautiful blessings are gifts
from our God, but nothing should come before Him. We should
entrust our families, our finances, our health, and our careers
to Him, and we should be so very grateful, but we are not to
worship anything other than our God. The wisdom of believing that He is truly sovereign and in control of our lives helps
us to deal with any fear, any wound, or any crisis that may be a
part of our journey. The feelings and circumstances will not be
sovereign, He will be. When we truly place our full trust in Him
and wholeheartedly believe that He is working all things for our
good, we can be filled with a sweet peace even in the darkest,
most painful times in our lives. The Bible tells us to be still and
know that He is God. We are to rest in His sovereignty. Even in
our darkest moments, we can rest in the beautiful truth that He
is with us and His strength will sustain us. We will not be alone.
Never alone.

When this really clicked and sealed in my heart, I realized that even if Glenn were to be unfaithful to me, reject me, leave me… I would not have to navigate through that pain by myself. My God… the God of Abraham, Isaac, and Jacob would have my back. Would have my heart. I would be able to handle the wound of grief with His help. He would hold my very life in the palm of His hand. He would be my helper. My anchor. My all in all! I finally let my precious Savior be my Lord as well. He became the alpha of my choices, and I found peace.

This knowledge changed my life! It gave me supernatural peace. He must be our first love… above everyone and everything. The beauty and the absolute truth are that when He is first, we make our choices based on truth and all the other areas are blessed! Our marriages, our relationships with our children, our careers, our finances, etc. We rest in the peace that we can pray and ask for help in any of these areas and the Creator of this universe will help us. How awesome is this knowledge! We don't have to navigate this world on our own. We are not alone on this journey. When we really get this, we will find true peace. True rest. True peace will fill our hearts and gratitude will overflow.

> *"What shall we say about such wonderful things as these? If God is for us, who can ever be against us? Since he did not spare even his own Son but gave him up for us all, won't he also give us everything else? Who dares accuse us whom God has chosen for his own? No one—for God himself has given us right standing with himself. Who then will condemn us? No one—for Christ Jesus died for us and was raised to life for us, and he is sitting in the place of honor at God's right hand, pleading for us.*

Can anything ever separate us from Christ's love? Does it mean he no longer loves us if we have trouble, or calamity, or are persecuted, or hungry, or destitute, or in danger, or threatened with death? (As the Scriptures say, 'For your sake we are killed every day; we are being slaughtered like sheep.') No, despite all these things, overwhelming victory is ours though Christ, who loved us.

And I am convinced that nothing can ever separate us from God's love. Neither death nor life, neither angels or demons, neither our fears for today nor our worries about tomorrow—not even the powers of hell can separate us from God's love. No power in the sky above or in the earth below-indeed, nothing in all creation will ever be able to separate us from the love of God that is revealed in Christ Jesus our Lord."

Romans 8:31-40

Now those words bring peace. Oh, how He loved us! Oh, how He loves us!

Oh, how happy Glenn was about my newfound knowledge! When I truly realized my worth and value was in my relationship with my Holy God through His precious Son Jesus, and I didn't rely on Glenn to provide it, beauty came, and it has remained. My heart overflows with gratitude to my Lord for His love, His sovereignty, and His peace. And Glenn is so grateful, too! I don't nag anymore, and he gets to live in peace with me. (He would say a big Amen right here.)

So, how do we let this peace overflow to others? We let others in. We share our love for Christ, we help those in need, and we become transparent in our walk. We let others know that we truly understand that it is not about us personally, but the living Christ within us.

Chapter 7
THE TRUTH

I find it both sad and sometimes humorous how many of us have spent most of our lives in the presence of other believers at church, and we smile and pretend that we are all put together and our families are like the ones in the sitcoms we used to watch long ago. However, if we are to truly love and encourage one another, it is time to be truthful. I don't mean to whine and moan so much that everyone runs away when they see us coming. I mean to get in small groups and share burdens and requests. We should be sharing each other's burdens and loads. This is how our mighty God designed us. If we as the church were reaching out as we should be, we would be shining like beacons of light to those around us who feel stifled by the darkness. There is so much darkness! Be the light. Shine His light and show His love.

My oldest granddaughter and I visited one of our city's homeless shelters for her 9th birthday. Her wish was to give a donation of needed items to the shelter and to give out cupcakes as a treat to the nightly residents. While we were distributing cupcakes, one of the ladies came up and proceeded to take off her necklace and give it to my granddaughter. The necklace was in the shape of a heart with a dove inside. We were both so moved. Her act of kindness was pure love in action. This lady was staying in a homeless shelter on a cold January day, and she was giving away all that she had to a stranger. Isn't this how we should be as ambassadors for Christ? Being generous with our things, our time, and our talents? In the book of Matthew, Jesus tells us that the two greatest commandments are to love our God and to love others, but are we? Are we really putting these into practice? Are we showing this cold, dark world the true meaning of genuine love?

> *"'Teacher, which is the most important commandment in the law of Moses?'*
>
> *Jesus replied, '"You must love the LORD your God with all your heart, all your soul, and all you mind." This is the first and greatest commandment. A second is equally important: "Love your neighbor as yourself." The entire law and all the demands of the prophets are based on these two commandments.'''*
>
> *Matthew 22:36-40*

What about pure and genuine religion? James 1:27 says, *"Pure and genuine religion in the sight of God the Father means caring for orphans and widows in their distress and refusing to let the world corrupt you."* Many of us in our culture today look to help someone who may be able to reward us for a good deed, but not so in this verse. I once heard a pastor say that the reason orphans and widows are mentioned here is because they have nothing to give back when helped except for love and gratitude. These are the very same things we can give our God. We can love Him and serve with a heart filled with gratitude. Are our motives pure in His eyes? When we bless others in His name, He receives the glory, and they see His love through us. This is truly loving our God and loving our neighbor.

There is a billboard for a local cable company near one of the roads I frequently travel, and it says something to the effect of, "We are building a culture that focuses on you." I believe this is one of our biggest problems as Christians. Our focus is too much on us, instead of our Jesus and instead of each other. I have failed at this so many times in my walk due to selfishness and fear, but I have learned that if we can put these in the right order, then we find peace.

If you were to ask me the greatest lesson I have learned on my journey, it would be to put God first in every area of my life. He should be our first love, and we should honor and obey Him with a Spirit-filled, grateful heart. This is true wisdom and the only way to an abundant life filled with joy.

Proverbs 3 is one of my favorite passages in the Bible as it lays out a life plan for those of us in Christ, and it tells us how very important it is to seek wisdom for our choices.

"My child, never forget the things I have taught you.
Store my commands in your heart.
If you do this, you will live many years,
and your life will be satisfying.
Never let loyalty and kindness leave you!
Tie them around your neck as a reminder.
Write them deep within your heart.
Then you will find favor with both God and people,
and you will earn a good reputation.

Trust in the LORD with all your heart;
do not depend on your own understanding.
Seek his will in all you do,
and he will show you which path to take.

Don't be impressed with your own wisdom.
Instead, fear the LORD and turn away from evil.
Then you will have healing for your body
and strength for your bones.

Honor the LORD with your wealth
and with the best part of everything you produce.
Then he will fill your barns with grain,
and your vats will overflow with good wine.

My child, don't reject the LORD'S discipline,
and don't be upset when he corrects you.
For the LORD corrects those he loves,
just as a father corrects a child in whom he delights.

Joyful is the person who finds wisdom,
the one who gains understanding.
For wisdom is more profitable than silver,
and her wages are better than gold.
Wisdom is more precious than rubies;
nothing you desire can compare with her.
She offers you long life in her right hand,
and riches and honor in her left.
She will guide you down delightful paths;
all her ways are satisfying.
Wisdom is a tree of life to those who embrace her;
happy are those who hold her tightly.

By wisdom the LORD founded the earth;
by understanding he created the heavens.
By his knowledge the deep fountains of the earth burst forth,
and the dew settles beneath the night sky.

My child, don't lose sight of common sense and discernment.
Hang on to them,
for they will refresh your soul.
They are like jewels on a necklace.
They keep you safe on your way,
and your feet will not stumble.
You can go to bed without fear;
you will lie down and sleep soundly.
You need not be afraid of sudden disaster
or the destruction that comes upon the wicked,
for the LORD is your security.
He will keep your foot from being caught in a trap."

Proverbs 3:1-26

I love that He is our security! I can live my daily life with the knowledge that my God is in control, and as I read His Word and draw near to Him, He will provide the wisdom and discernment that I will need to live out His purpose and fulfill His commission. It is so important that we understand that this is a daily walk and not a weekly visit to church for an hour. Branches don't visit a tree once a week for the nourishment they need. They remain with the tree, and they are nurtured and find their life source there. He is the vine, and we are the branches, and we need to be rooted in His Word, His wisdom, and His discernment. These beautiful roots will also hold us steady in the roughest storms that may arise and help us to be still in His presence as the storm rages.

Powerful words from our Jesus:

"Remain in me, and I will remain in you. For a branch cannot produce fruit if it is severed from the vine, and you cannot be fruitful unless you remain in me.

Yes, I am the vine; you are the branches. Those who remain in me, and I in them, will produce much fruit. For apart from me you can do nothing. Anyone who does not remain in me is thrown away like a useless branch and withers. Such branches are gathered into a pile to be burned. But if you remain in me and my words remain in you, you may ask for anything you want, and it will be granted! When you produce much fruit, you are my true disciples. This brings glory to my Father.

I have loved you even as the Father has loved me. Remain in my love. When you obey my commandments, you remain in my love, just as I obey my Father's commandments and remain in his love. I have told you these things so that you will be filled with my joy. Yes, your joy will overflow! This is my commandment: Love each other in the same way I have loved you. There is no greater love than to lay down one's life for one's friends. You are my friends if you do what I command. I no longer call you slaves, because a master doesn't confide in his slaves. Now you are my friends, since I have told you everything the Father told me. You didn't choose me. I chose you. I appointed you to go and produce lasting fruit, so that the Father will give you whatever you ask for, using my name. This is my command: Love each other."

John 15:4-17

The other part of my life lesson is that there is no good in me except for my Jesus. Ephesians 2:8-9 says, *"God saved you by his grace when you believed. And you can't take credit for this; it is a gift from God. Salvation is not a reward for the good things we have done, so none of us can boast about it."* Oh, how this comforts my soul and frees me to love our God with a grateful heart and not a fearful one. He knew what my choices would be, even while I was still in my mother's womb, and He has loved me from my conception despite them. My sweet friend, God's love for you is not based on your choices either. His love is unconditional because He is love and He is your mighty Creator. He is the reason you were born. How beautiful to know that we are so loved! Now our job as His ambassadors is to glorify Him by placing Him first in our lives and showing His love to those around us. We are to do good in His name and draw others to Him. We are each placed in strategic places to reach those around us, and if we all work together to show God's love, we will celebrate in Heaven one day with those we have reached.

Is this difficult sometimes? Yes, it is, but we are not His ambassadors through our own strength, but through His. Seek Him, ask for wisdom, and then fulfill your commission. It is time for us to speak out and reach the lost and searching souls around us. It is time to speak hope into the lives of those who feel hopeless and life into those who feel they have no life. It is time to get real!

R – Relationship: Our entire faith walk should be based on a personal relationship with Jesus Christ and His biblical scriptural wisdom. Our hearts should overflow with gratitude to our Father God for loving us so much that He gave His only begotten Son, that whosoever believeth on Him should not perish, but have eternal life.

E – Evangelism: We are His ambassadors, and we have been commissioned to spread the gospel by shining His light to those around us. This is true evangelism. Let us work together to do this as the body of Christ. Can you imagine what this world would look like if each of us reached out and worked together as a collective body of believers to spread the gospel and share His love?

A – All in: We are to be all in. Either we believe that our Holy God sent His precious Son Jesus Christ to be a sacrifice for us and we put Him first in each of our choices, or we are floundering and trying to live this life on our own. Choose Jesus. Choose peace.

L – Love: Our entire commission is to be pursued in love. Love of our Creator, our Savior, and the sweet Holy Spirit. We can do this with the full knowledge of how very much we are loved, and when we truly understand this, we can love others as we should. Through His eyes, through the filter of His Word.

We can begin this process of being real by speaking hope to those in our families. Have you noticed that sometimes we are meaner to the people we love the most? Let's vow to begin our commission of love and kindness with those closest to us. Our spouse, our children, our parents, and our brothers and sisters. Life is hard on our families of today. Our enemy will try anything to destroy our families, and we need to be on guard. The Bible tells us to do so. We stay on guard by reading and studying the Holy Scriptures and praying, and we show love by our words and actions. Show love while making dinner after a hard day at work, show love while doing homework with your babies, show love while cleaning your house, show love while driving in the car. (Please wave with all five fingers when someone else isn't driving so well.)

Speak the truth in love and listen with love. Sometimes, the most loving thing we can do for others is simply listen. Everyone needs to feel heard, loved, and appreciated. When we feel like we have nothing left to give, we need to go to Him for more. He is our portion. He is our strength. We cannot do this on our own, and personally, I can tell when I am trying to handle this life in my own strength. I feel more irritable or weepy, and much more overwhelmed by the cares of this world, and I am far less compassionate and much more critical of others. I need to stay rooted in Him daily by reading His Word and praying with a grateful heart in order to glorify Him with my choices and abide in His peace. Again, we must remember that this is a daily walk and not just a weekly fill up. Let us walk wisely, my friend.

Chapter 8

THE TREASURES

I began my story with the sadness of loss and the darkness of grief. I will end this part of my story with the joy of new life and the birth of my sweet granddaughter, Aria. I witnessed her birth today, and I watched as she took her first breath here on earth. She is my third grandchild, and my heart overflows with gratitude when I think of how good God is to me.

I want my grandchildren to learn how much they are loved by our Creator. I want them to learn early in their lives how very important it is to trust and lean on their Savior, and I now realize how very crucial our jobs as parents and grandparents truly are. I pray for them to gain wisdom and walk in God's truths, and it is our job to guide them to these truths.

"And you must love the Lord your God with all your heart, all your soul, and all your strength. And you must commit yourselves wholeheartedly to these commands that I am giving you today. Repeat them again and again to your children. Talk about them when you are at home and when you are on the road, when you are going to bed and when you are getting up. Tie them to your hands and wear them on your forehead as reminders. Write them on the doorposts of your house and on your gates."

Deuteronomy 6:5-9

What an enormous responsibility we have! So many of our children today are struggling with feelings of inadequacy and loneliness. So many are turning to social media for validation and affirmation. We are losing them to the worries of this world when we need to be teaching them that they can have the Spirit of the Most-High God inside and they will not be alone. I so wish that I had known this wisdom when I was a young mom.

How beautiful when we empower them with the knowledge that our God knew them in the womb and He knew all their days before they were born. Nothing surprises our God. They are fearfully and wonderfully made in His image, and His love for them far outweighs the opinions of others. When our children truly understand how much they are loved and that they are never alone, they can maneuver through this world with the confidence that they can do anything through Him. There is also beauty in knowing that He is enough. He is our all. He is our peace. They do not have to turn to drugs, alcohol, promiscuity, or any other worldly vice to ease the pain or loneliness that they may experience on their journey. They can turn to their Savior, and He will comfort them and guide them to healing and peace.

"I can do everything through Christ, who gives me strength."
Philippians 4:13

You may be wondering why I have written about our responsibilities as parents. I wrote in the beginning of my story how much I hope for you to learn from my missteps. During the awful time after my first husband left and the years of my second marriage, most of my actions were motivated by a selfish sense of emotional survival. I was searching for the internal peace that only full surrender to my Jesus could offer, but my focus was mainly on me. I have deep regrets about not being the mom that I should have been to Ashley and the choices that I made when she was younger. Our sins, although forgiven, will bring consequences not only to us, but sadly, sometimes to those we love the most. I fully understand the importance of being present with our children now. This life is hard, and it is so easy for parents to lose focus of what is truly important and eternal. The souls of our children. The nurturing of their souls and the time and discipline that it takes to do so. Be present, my friend. Tell them often how much they are loved by God and by you. Speak of stories that promote empathy for others. Model Christ's love for others for them to see, and discipline them in love, not anger. There will be times when we all mess up, but the Bible tells us that love covers a multitude of sins. Love them and let them see you showing love to others.

I so wish that I had hearkened to God's Word when I was younger and that I had known the extreme importance of obedience to my Lord. The following verse helps me to realize the full impact of the importance of my obedience and my walk. I only want the best for those I love, and I am sure you do as well. We need to be conscious of the fact that our choices affect our children and our children's children and beyond. Let us remember this as we navigate this world as adults. Let us be wise and cherish these beautiful blessings from God.

"Observe and obey all these words which I command you, that it may go well with you and your children after you forever, when you do what is good and right in the sight of the LORD your God."
Deuteronomy 12:28 (NKJV)

It is so important that our little ones learn how very much they are loved by God. There is a supernatural peace that comes with this understanding. When they truly understand how precious they are in God's sight, they will begin to live with the reassurance that they are not alone in the darkness of their rooms at night, or when they are playing at a friend's house and mom and dad are not there. When they enter school, and everything is different and scary. When they feel left out or mistreated by others. The beauty of knowing God's love will then abide in their hearts as they grow older and comfort them when they face everyday challenges, including disappointments, failures, and heartaches. They will know that they are valued and truly loved by their Creator and He has a plan and purpose for their lives. Our children need to feel special, cherished, and loved.

So many of our children today have no true understanding that they are not alone. They are feeling that their worth is based on a friend's opinion or how they are received on social media. So how do we combat this? Immerse them in the Scriptures. Teach them that they are fearfully and wonderfully made, and that they are unique and loved. Tell them Bible stories of how God protected and empowered those who trusted in Him. Speak to them about angels and how God wants to protect them just as you do as their parent. Let them see the priority that you place in your faith. Let them see you walk with the beautiful assurance that God is in control.

Our children must also understand how very deeply they are loved by us. These precious little ones must learn what love looks like from us. Not just our words, but true love in action. Unconditional love and self-sacrifice modeled just as our Jesus modeled for us. We must put down our phones and speak to our children, listen to them, and spend time playing with them. They should feel how much they are loved simply by their presence in our midst. You may be surprised how much your children will speak of unknown worries or concerns during play, and this sharing will help you to have insight into the areas where they may be struggling.

Our children need to feel safe and secure. They need to understand that we are their earthly protectors, and they can rest in the knowledge that we will be there. In situations of divorce, children need to understand that they can abide in the knowledge that both parents still love them, even though the structure of the family will be different. In the case of abandonment by one parent, please do not down the absent parent. Let your children know that grown-ups can make some very hurtful choices, but still have love in their hearts for their children. Saying bad things about an absent parent will only cause more hurt and confusion for your child, and it is wrong and unbiblical. Do your best to create a harmonious and positive family structure for your babies. Ask our Lord to help you to be Christ-like in your dealings with the changes that occur in divorce. He can help you, and only through Him can love be shown in these sad changes. Look to Him in your pain and anger, and through Him help your children to feel safe in the storm. I took my eyes off of my Jesus and focused on my pain, and my sweet daughter suffered for it. Please don't do the same.

Our children also need structure in their everyday lives. They need specific guidelines to help them to feel safe. They need to know there is a time to eat, to play, to nap if age appropriate, and a time for quality time with you. The time with you is paramount in helping them to feel loved and secure. Time together will build beautiful memories that you and they will cherish for a lifetime. In each family, this will look different, but please take the time to make it work for you. One of the sad tragedies of this world is that we get so caught up in "life" … work, bills, obligations, that we lose sight of the most important things. Time with God, time with our spouse, and time with our precious children. Please do not give all your energy to this outside world and have nothing left for your family. I have been there, and I have deep regrets. Fix your eyes on Jesus and ask Him to help you to rest in Him as you show love to the people that He has gifted you with in your home, and then use your energy for ministry outside of your home. One more note on time with your family. Many families today have so many after school activities that our children are drowning in busyness. Slow down. I understand that we want our children to excel in the activities that they are gifted in, but what is our number one priority as parents? To raise a pro athlete? To raise a celebrity? No, sweet friend, our children are a gift from our Holy God, and He has entrusted us with the huge responsibility of raising our children to love Him with all of their heart, soul, mind, and strength.

Think about it…even after they graduate from high school or college and get their dream job, what then? Make money, live the American dream? I love this great country, but our only dream for our children shouldn't be that they grow up, go to college, get married and have babies of their own. That is not our commission! Our commission is to teach them to love God and to live a life seeking His wisdom and obeying His commands. In this is their true joy! In this is true life! If they are honoring God and putting Him first in all they do, then they are living the dream. God's dream and God's plan for them. How beautiful for us as parents and grandparents if we can see our precious loved ones living in peace and joy, even in the midst of the everyday struggles of this world! So how do we do this?

We go back to Deuteronomy and we speak life into them from infants. We model God's love, and we let them know that God's rules for us are there to keep us safe. We teach them to love God's parameters and that rebellion can cause us personal harm, and it can also affect others. Our responsibility as parents is to teach our children that their behavioral choices should be based on biblical principles and that they should seek wisdom from God when making them. We teach them from a young age to live with integrity, and we speak of it often. We teach them to be kind to others, even if they disagree with them. There should be no room for hate in our children's lives. Or ours. We teach them that there will be hard times in their lives when things do not seem to make sense, and we teach them to pray, trust, and seek wise counsel during those times. We teach them that God is the light in their darkness. Whether this be a bully at school, a teenage crush that brings hurt, or issues with friends while growing up. They must know in their hearts that their Heavenly Father is working all things for their good. They must know that they are not alone.

My grandchildren spent the night with Glenn and I last night and, during their visit, we watched the movie *Trolls*. The main character in the movie is Poppy and she is extremely positive, and this is inspirational for many of the other characters but not Branch. He has experienced much sorrow in his past, and he is very bitter. Branch confronts Poppy in the movie about her believing that the world is all cupcakes and rainbows. After watching that scene, my grandson Canon turned to me and said he was sad. When I asked why, he replied, "Because the world is not all cupcakes and rainbows." Truer words have never been spoken by a five-year-old. This gave me a teachable moment with this precious grandson, whose very presence brings me joy, to let him know that, although the statement was true, the Bible tells us that we always have hope and even in the sad times we can know that we are loved, and beauty is coming. Use your moments, sweet friend. They will accrue into knowledge and wisdom for our little ones, and you will be honoring God with your most important treasures.

As adults, we also need to believe that, even in our storms, a rainbow is coming. We can dream of the cupcakes and hope for the rainbows. Many of us simply live on dreams and do not believe there is hope. My friend, there is always hope. Do not look at your circumstances. Look to the One who has the power to help change your circumstances. The One who has the power to give you peace and strength during the hardest trials in your circumstances. Look to the One who loves you with an everlasting love and who is waiting for you to call out. To acknowledge Him. To simply ask for help. To simply ask for relief. For peace. For wisdom. Call out, sweet friend. Call out.

Chapter 9

THE MESSAGE FOR OUR MIDDLE

I had planned to bring you to the current day in my journey by telling you that Ashley is now a flight attendant and how our God has brought her full circle by using her childhood love of flying. This love was discovered each summer when she would visit her father in Florida (He and his new wife had moved back there soon after our divorce). She would fly unaccompanied from our home to his. The flight attendants had the responsibility of keeping her safe and they had my total trust.

However, she is not yet a flight attendant. She was due to graduate from training six days ago but was sent home early from training. This was due to the virus that is currently plaguing our great land and beyond. Ashley is currently enjoying being a stay-at-home mom and waiting until the airlines are back to full capacity in their operations. She will then go back to finish training and begin a new career and a new portion of her journey. This could be a very scary and disconcerting time as her mom, but I am hopeful, and each day brings joy. I see the beauty in the extra time with her children. She has two of her own now. Canon is five and Aria is three, and they are loving having their sweet mom at home! She also has a daughter whom she has been entrusted with by her husband.

Her stepdaughter Kadence, who is twelve. My prayer is that Ashley uses the lessons learned in her blended family experience to help Kadence to feel loved and cherished as each little one should. Ashley's husband leads the music worship at their church, and she sings with him frequently. She also helps with the youth's music worship. She loves her little family and seeing her as a mom brings joy to my heart and gratitude deep in my soul. I do not know what the future holds for my sweet girl and her family, but I know who holds their future, and I know who holds mine and yours as well. Therein is our peace.

> *"Don't worry about anything; instead pray about everything. Tell God what you need, and thank him for all he has done. Then you will experience God's peace, which exceeds anything we can understand. His peace will guard your hearts and minds as you live in Christ Jesus."*
>
> *Philippians 4:6-7*

Currently, this virus has our nation under quarantine and there is death and suffering all around. There is also a large amount of fear due to the rapid spread of the virus. In addition to this, the self-distancing protocols that have been put in place to help us have closed many businesses and put thousands out of work. With no income, fear and anxiety have risen to new levels in our country and throughout our world. Illness, death, and suffering have stirred up many fears and they are the focus of our national news at this time. If we were to only look around, this could become emotionally overwhelming.

There is also a racial unrest that is dividing our nation. Instead of seeing each other as individuals, our enemy is using hatred and violence to separate entire groups of people. Therefore, we are not to just look around. We are to look up. We are to look within our Bibles to gain knowledge, peace, and wisdom. If we do this, we will find power and strength and then be able to live with a joy-filled heart even in the midst of uncertainty. Our hearts are saddened for those who have lost loved ones and for those who are in need during these crises, but we will not fear. We will walk with the assurance that the most powerful force in the universe lives inside of us and He is in control. Not the virus, not the government, not the enemy! Our God is. Hold your head up daughter of the Most High. He is our Abba Father, and He is working on our behalf.

If you are one of the thousands who have been touched by grief during this dark period, please know that you are loved and that your loss has touched our hearts. Many, many prayers have been spoken for you and your family even though we do not know your name. We know that you have experienced tremendous loss and pain and that is why we have prayed for comfort and strength for you from the only One who can provide it. He sees you sweet friend, and He knows your name, and He sees your pain. Let Him in. Let Him wrap His arms around you and carry you through the dark veil of grief and let His love and comfort be a balm to your wounds. He is your light in the darkness.

Amidst the current chaos we see on the news, we are also seeing stories of beauty and hope. Stories of essential workers being honored for their courage and compassion and strength. This is love in action! As Christians, we are to show our Savior's love to a hurting world. If we would just open our eyes, we would see Him working through His children and this would encourage us and bring hope to us and to others. We all need hope, and we need to be spreading it in His name.

There are many movies that share true stories of hope and I find the movie *42* beautiful and inspiring. The language is a little rough, but each of our stories is filled with "a little rough" of something, and this man's story is one of true courage and perseverance. The movie is about Jackie Robinson, who was the first African American man to play major league baseball. As I watched his story on the small screen, I was inspired by his courage and determination to follow his dream, even in the face of extreme opposition and even hatred. I thought about my life as a parallel to baseball and how we are all running our race, living in this game of life. We are up to bat thousands of times during our lifetimes, and we must make critical choices each time.

With God's help we can get on base or even steal home. There are also many times that we strike out or are tagged out in this game. We can wallow in our defeats, or we can ask for help from our Heavenly Father and from those He places in our lives and we can press on. As believers, we are on a team. A team of witnesses for our Jesus, and we are to work together to share the gospel and shine His light. We will have innings of beauty, innings of sorrow, and even innings of the unknown, but we can make it through each one with His help. When we give Him first place as our manager and coach, we can rest in His perfect peace even though our game may be fraught with tension, disruption, and unexpected plays. We will be a victor in this game, and we will be playing until we reach our beautiful eternal "home."

Before leaving on a long road trip with his team, Jackie Robinson would say to his wife, "You are in my heart." I found this to be beautiful. As Christians, we carry the Holy Spirit of God in our hearts. Let us really process this for a moment. The most powerful force in the universe lives in our hearts and He goes everywhere with us, and yet we still hesitate or even fail to live out our faith. I have failed so many times, my friend, and during the darkest inning of my life, I actually struck out for a period of time. But God... He did not let me lose. He gave me another "at bat." He wiped away the dust from my uniform, He helped me rise with His righteous right hand, and I am still a player in this game. This beautiful knowledge makes my heart swell with gratitude to my Savior, my Lord, and helps me to live in this sin-darkened world with a continual attitude of prayer and communion with the One who brings light.

We are not alone, and it is time that we live in victory and let others see Him through us. We are to be His hands and feet. A voice for the poor and the needy and an advocate for those who are oppressed. He is in our hearts and He wants to be seen and wants to be heard. It is up to our team to spread His love and spread His Word to a hurting and searching world. It is time to get off the bench and show up. I refuse to sit it out or forfeit anymore. Let us join together and win precious souls for our Holy God, who has given so much for us!

In this movie, many of the other players on Jackie's team and the other teams as well were against his playing ball with them because of his race. However, when they started to see him as an individual instead of a stereotypical figure of their targeted racism and hatred, their hearts started to change. Oh, how our hearts need to be changed! Not only are we to represent Him, but we are to see others as He sees them. We may have many differences with others, but we are all part of the human race and we are to be salt and light in this world. It is time to work together as a team. A team of believers who love Jesus and who are committed to loving our neighbors the way the Bible commands. As we do this, let's remember to give each other grace. Remember, grace is undeserved favor, and we need to view others through the lens of His grace. The irritable clerk at the store may have unpaid bills that are weighing on her mind. The man in his car, who is riding your car's bumper, may have just received news about a family member who has been taken to the hospital. The edge in the tone of the person on the phone, may have absolutely nothing to do with you. We all have difficult days and we mess up. Try to see others through His eyes and this will help you and those around you to abide in peace. I think the famous actress Audrey Hepburn understood this when she said…

"For beautiful eyes, look for the good in others; for beautiful lips, speak only words of kindness; and for poise, walk with the knowledge that you are never alone."

Never alone. It is time, sweet Christian friend, to find life through Him and to start really living! Live for Him and let Him live through you. Find your joy and live in His peace. Let Him be your center and your Lord.

I am so grateful to be on His team with you! Let's head for home plate, knowing that He is in our hearts. We can rest assured, with Him as our coach, we will be victorious! In fact, the Bible tells us that we already are.

"Praise the LORD!

How joyful are those who fear the LORD
and delight in obeying his commands.
Their children will be successful everywhere;
an entire generation of godly people will be blessed.
They themselves will be wealthy,

and their good deeds will last forever.
Light shines in the darkness for the godly.
They are generous, compassionate, and righteous.
Good comes to those who lend money generously
and conduct their business fairly.
Such people will not be overcome by evil.
Those who are righteous will be remembered.
They do not fear bad news;
they confidently trust the LORD to care for them.
They are confident and fearless
and can face their foes triumphantly.
They share freely and give generously to those in need.
Their good deeds will be remembered forever.
They will have influence and honor."

Psalm 112:1-9

I have seen and felt many things throughout the years of my journey. Some have been beautiful and some things I would like to forget, but through it all, my God has been faithful. I will praise His name at all times! I will look to Him for help, wisdom, and guidance and I will not be foolish and try to live this life on my own again. I don't want to be weak anymore. I don't want to be on the wrong team anymore. I want to be a vessel for Him. To be strong in Him. To glorify Him. May His Holy Word be a constant lamp unto my feet and a light unto my path on my journey. And for your journey too!

"I look up to the mountain—
does my help come from there?
My help comes from the LORD,
who made heaven and earth!

He will not let you stumble;
the one who watches over you will not slumber.
Indeed, he who watches over Israel
never slumbers or sleeps.

The LORD himself watches over you!
The LORD stands beside you as your protective shade.
The sun will not harm you by day,
nor the moon at night.

The LORD keeps you from all harm
and watches over your life.
The LORD keeps watch over you as you come and go,
both now and forever."

Psalm 121

He is watching over us even now, and His arms are open wide. His beautiful eyes are full of compassion, and we are so loved! Rejoice and rest, sweet friend, in His goodness. Walk with boldness and stand firm in your faith! Let Him be your first love and then His love will permeate your heart, and His love and light will shine on those whom you love. His peace will be with you wherever you go, and this supernatural peace will be able to center you through whatever circumstances may arise on your journey. Let Him be your anchor in your storms.

"Whoever pursues righteousness and unfailing love will find life,
righteousness, and honor."

Proverbs 21:21

This proverb is one of my favorite verses in the Bible. I believe that if each of us in the body of believers was truly pursuing righteousness and unfailing love, we could be life changers and even world changers for our Jesus in this sin-darkened world. It is time for us to live out our commission and show our Jesus to our families and to the hurting and lost around us. This is real life, and it is time that we started really living. In our homes, in our schools, in our hospitals, in our offices, in our cars, wherever we are. Real life. True life. In Him. It really is all about Him! Go find your life, sweet friend. Your beautiful, God-given life. He will be with you, and you will never be alone. Read and study His Word, live in a spirit of prayer, ask for wisdom and discernment, obey His teachings, and above all, love. Love Him and love others. We all need to love more and rest in the beautiful peace that He is near, and He truly cares for each of us.

The Bible tells us that our sovereign God does not slumber or sleep. His eyes roam throughout the Earth looking for those who are seeking Him and trying to do what is right in His eyes. You are seen, and you are loved today. Even when you may feel alone, you are not. He is the Alpha and the Omega. The beginning and the end. Your beginning and your end. Please let Him be on the throne of your heart in the middle!

"Then I saw a new heaven and a new earth, for the old heaven and the old earth had disappeared. And the sea was also gone. And I saw the holy city, the new Jerusalem, coming down from God out of heaven like a bride beautifully dressed for her husband.

I heard a loud shout from the throne, saying, 'Look, God's home is now among his people! He will live with them, and they will be his people. God himself will be with them. He will wipe every tear from their eyes, and there will be no more death or sorrow or crying or pain. All these things are gone forever!'

And the one sitting on the throne said, 'Look, I am making everything new!' And then he said to me, 'Write this down, for what I tell you is trustworthy and true.' And he also said, 'It is finished! I am the Alpha and the Omega—the Beginning and the End. To all who are thirsty I will give freely from the springs of the water of life. All who are victorious will inherit all these blessings, and I will be their God, and they will be my children.'"

Revelation 21:1-7

"Look, I am coming soon, bringing my reward with me to repay all people according to their deeds. I am the Alpha and the Omega, the First and the Last, the Beginning and the End."

Revelation 22:12-13

I pray, Father, in the name of your precious Son Jesus, that as individuals and as a body of believers, we make the middle count. Please give us the courage to do this with You as our beginning, our Alpha. The beginning of our thoughts, our actions, and our reactions to others. Let us look to You for needed wisdom and discernment as we travel on our way, and please renew us with Your strength and Your peace each moment of every day. Let us find our life in You. Real life in You. Let us live for You, dear God. For Your glory. All for You, Father. All for You. Oh, how we love you! Amen.

As you finish reading my story today, I would encourage you sweet friend, to give Him the leading role in yours. Know that you are seen, and you are known by your Holy Creator, and you are so very loved by the One who gave you life. Now it is your turn to live your life as an offering of thanksgiving to Him. A beautiful, joy-filled offering of gratitude. We will be grateful together, and I wish you beauty on your journey!

I Want to Know You
By Ashley Tannahill

Who am I and what am I here for?
The question rings in my head
And how can it be there's something greater than what I see
    lies ahead?
I swam through the storms and fought through the fights
But I never thought You could be so right

I want to know You
The Author of My Soul
The One with everything to make me whole
So, let me know You with everything I am
From the beginning to the end
And who are You?
The One who holds the stars in His hands
The One who set out on a journey and died
Yes, died for me in the end
But it's not the end
For You rose again to save my soul and make me whole

I want to know You
The Author of My Soul
The One with everything to make me whole
So, let me know You with everything I am
From the beginning to the end

And I know it may be hard, when I feel like I'm alone, but deep
    inside I know You're still here
My heart's your home

I want to know You
The Author of My Soul
The One with everything to make me whole
So, let me know You with everything I am
From the beginning to the end

From the beginning to the end
Let me know You

CPSIA information can be obtained
at www.ICGtesting.com
Printed in the USA
LVHW021620280521
688802LV00017B/594

9 781637 692042